YOUNG ZOOLOGIST
HUMPBACK WHALE

A FIRST FIELD GUIDE TO THE SINGING GIANT OF THE OCEAN

CONTENTS

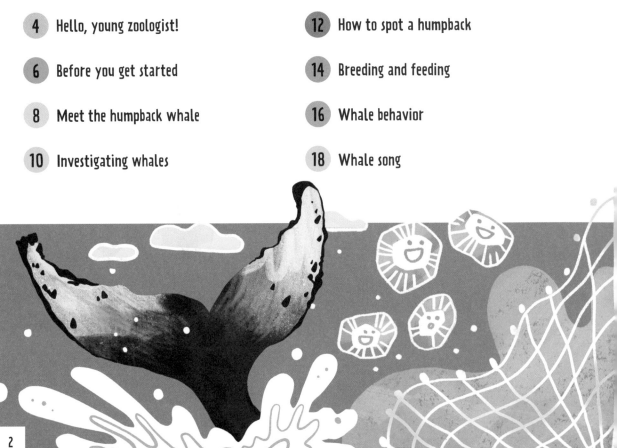

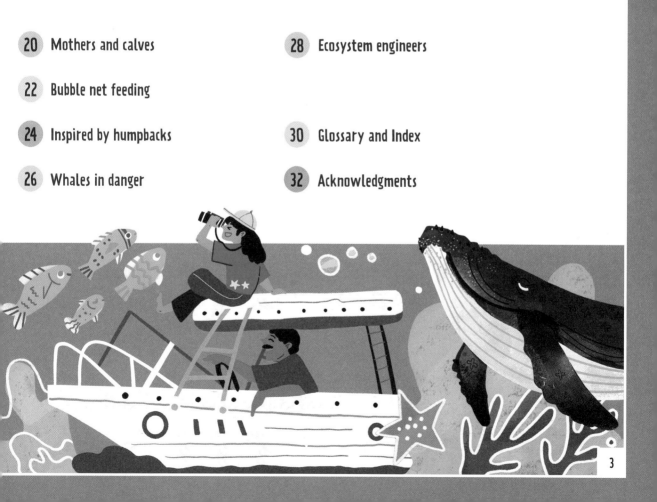

HELLO, YOUNG ZOOLOGIST!

My name is Dr. Asha de Vos. I am a Sri Lankan marine biologist and your personal whale guide on this adventure. I love humpback whales. As a scientist who studies whale behavior, I believe that humpbacks have a lot to offer.

Have you ever met a humpback whale? Yes? How lucky! No? No problem. Let's explore this magnificent animal together, so when you do meet one you will be armed with lots of fantastic facts.

I'm ready to go exploring! Are you?

DR. ASHA DE VOS

FACT FILE

SCIENTIFIC NAME
Megaptera novaeangliae

TYPE
Mammal

FAMILY
Whales

HABITAT
Oceans worldwide

WEIGHT
88,000 lb (40,000 kg)

EATS
Krill and small fish

CONSERVATION STATUS
Least concern

SIZE COMPARISON

HUMPBACK
52 ft (16 m)

BLUE WHALE
82 ft (25 m)

SPERM WHALE
52 ft (16 m)

MINKE WHALE
30 ft (9 m)

ORCA
26 ft (8 m)

BELUGA
13 ft (4 m)

HUMAN
6 ft (1.8 m)

5

BEFORE YOU GET STARTED

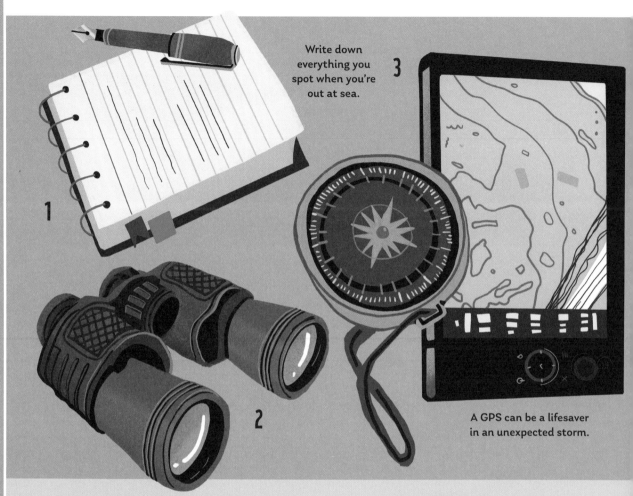

Write down everything you spot when you're out at sea.

A GPS can be a lifesaver in an unexpected storm.

1 **NOTEBOOK AND PEN**
You never know when something might happen, so you should always be prepared to write it down. You should also make a note of the date, location, weather, and anything else that helps you remember the day.

2 **BINOCULARS**
The ocean is so huge that everything in it seems small. A pair of binoculars lets you see distant objects more closely. They're especially handy for looking at small details on the whales you are watching.

3 **GPS AND COMPASS**
A GPS (Global Positioning System) uses satellites to figure out where in the world you are. Since the ocean has no landmarks, you can use GPS to plan where you want to go and how you will get there. If you don't have GPS, a compass can help you find your way.

Turning a whale-watching trip into a scientific expedition is easy. First, pick a question you want to answer, such as, "What kind of whale visits this area?" Then grab some gear and head out to investigate!

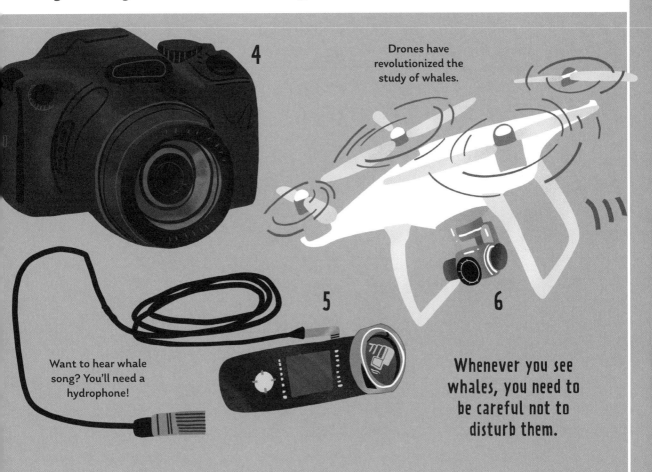

4

Drones have revolutionized the study of whales.

5

6

Want to hear whale song? You'll need a hydrophone!

Whenever you see whales, you need to be careful not to disturb them.

4 CAMERA
This simple but powerful tool can help unravel many ocean mysteries. You can take photos of whales to identify them later, which can help you get to know the individuals that visit the area regularly.

5 HYDROPHONE
This underwater microphone is waterproofed and ready to go! You can use it to listen to the sounds beneath the surface of the ocean, like chatting whales or the noise of boats and ships.

6 DRONE
A drone is like having a camera in the sky. Using one lets you watch whales from a unique angle, study how they swim through the ocean, and look out for other exciting marine life.

MEET THE HUMPBACK WHALE

Say hello to one of the giants of the ocean. Humpback whales get their name from the little hump in front of their dorsal fin. Can you see it? They weigh as much as five African elephants and have *huge* appetites.

DORSAL FIN

This knobby fin is located halfway along the whale's back.

TAIL

The tail is the engine of this giant. By moving it up and down, the whale can propel itself through the ocean.

Humpback whales are about the size of a school bus.

SKELETON

Whales have fewer bones than humans because they don't have legs or feet. While adult humans have 206 bones, humpbacks have around 161.

PECTORAL FLIPPERS

These flippers are used for swimming in shallow water, speeding up quickly, changing direction, and shoving fish into the whale's mouth.

Humpback whales are found in every ocean on Earth.

BLOWHOLES

Humpback whales aren't fish—they're mammals (like you) who can't breathe underwater. They have a pair of giant nostrils at the top of their head, which they close when they're diving.

When a humpback surfaces it releases air from its blowholes.

MOUTH

Humpback whales don't have teeth. They have comblike bristles, called baleen, that line their upper jaws.

The thick bristles are perfect for trapping food.

SKIN

Humpbacks often have hitchhikers in the form of thousands of barnacles! They fix themselves to the whale's skin and get carried around the ocean to the best feeding spots.

9

INVESTIGATING WHALES

Studying dead humpback whales that wash ashore can tell scientists a lot about the lives of these mysterious creatures—and the animals that like to feast on them. Let's take a closer look.

Inside the ear

EARWAX

Whale earwax builds up in layers, one layer every year. Over time these growth layers form an ear plug. By counting the layers we can estimate the age of the whale.

The carrot-shaped part is the whale's earwax plug.

Count the growth layers (lines) to see how old this whale is!

TASTY BONES

Osedax worms tunnel into the bones of dead whales in the deepest parts of our oceans. They like to feast on the tasty oils inside. Weirdly, the worms that land on the bones of whales are all female!

A worm feasting on bone

OLD BALEEN

Bristly baleen acts like a journal of a whale's life. Studying baleen can tell scientists whether an individual faced a threat, became pregnant, or swam in polluted waters.

Baleen is made from keratin—just like your hair and nails.

HOW TO SPOT A HUMPBACK

How do you spot a humpback when you are out at sea or sitting on a cliff staring at the ocean? Here are some tips about what to look for and how to make sure you aren't looking at another type of whale.

SURFACING

When a humpback comes up for a breath, you may only see its back. Quick—does it have a hump in front of its dorsal fin? Is the whale black and white? If so, you're probably looking at a humpback!

DIVING

When a whale dives, it arches its back high and slithers into the ocean, often silently. Humpbacks lift their tail flukes high into the air and wave goodbye as they descend to the depths.

BLOWING

Whales must come to the surface of the ocean to breathe. They stay there for a few minutes breathing out and in, or blowing, until it's time to dive again. Humpback spray is shaped like a bush or a cloud.

FLUKES

Just like your fingerprints are unique to you, no two humpbacks have the same tail flukes. The scars and marks allow us to recognize individuals so we can learn where they go and even how old they are. Humpback flukes are broad and curvy.

Try to sketch the patterns you see on the flukes.

Left fluke

Trailing edge

Notch

Right fluke

Fluke tip

Leading edge

Use these terms to describe where you spot the patterns on a humpback's flukes.

Scars can be caused by other animals, such as orcas, or collisions with boats or fishing gear.

13

BREEDING AND FEEDING

- - - - - - - - →

MIGRATION ROUTES

Every year humpback whales travel vast distances between cooler areas that have more food and their breeding grounds in the tropics.

BREEDING GROUNDS

Humpbacks give birth in the safety of shallow tropical waters. The mothers and calves remain there until the calf is big and strong enough to make the long swim to the feeding grounds.

FEEDING GROUNDS

Feeding grounds are like gigantic fridges filled with a whale's favorite food! Humpbacks gather here to feast on krill (shrimplike creatures) and small fish.

The Arabian Sea humpback whales are the only humpback population that does not migrate.

Where do humpback whales meet their partners, have babies, and feed? Everywhere! But humpbacks don't all go to the same places. Instead, each population has its own preferred feeding and breeding grounds that they travel, or migrate, between during the year.

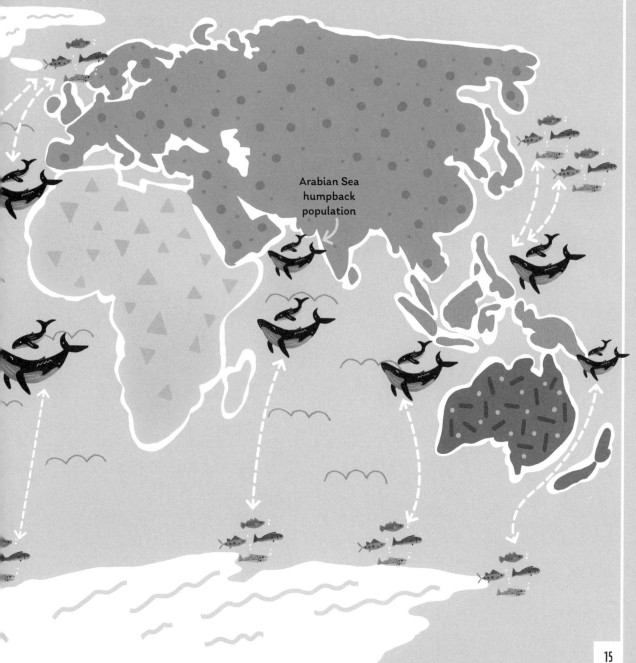

Arabian Sea humpback population

WHALE BEHAVIOR

PEC SLAPPING

A humpback whale might smack the water with one or both of its pectoral flippers at the same time, making a loud *SLAP!* sound. Scientists believe that humpbacks pec slap to communicate with one another.

BREACHING

To see a whale breach is to witness magic. This giant of our oceans propels itself completely out of the water using the power of its tail. It does this either to remove pesky parasites attached to its skin, to communicate with others farther away, or—in the case of younger whales—for fun!

The best way to learn about any animal is to watch how it behaves. What does it eat? How does it move? Does it spend time with others or alone? Humpback whales have a range of behaviors that can tell us more about their secret lives.

SPYHOPPING

This is like a game of "now you see me, now you don't." Humpbacks will gently (and silently) poke their heads vertically out of the water to look at the world around them and then, just as gently, slip back in.

HEAD LUNGING

This competitive display sees the whale lunging forward with its head raised above the water, before falling forward on its chin! The loud splash sends a message to anyone around it.

WHALE SONG

All humpback whales use sound to communicate, but it's only the males that sing. Their songs are complex and haunting to hear. Did you know that each population of humpback whales has a different song? Cool, huh?

SINGING FOR A MATE

Humpback males hang vertically upside down when they sing, sometimes for hours! Because they sing during the mating season, the song may be used to attract a girlfriend or to warn the other males that they are bigger and stronger.

SONG STRUCTURE

Songs are made up of units—moans, cries, chirps—that are arranged into phrases. Lots of phrases repeated make themes. Stick a few themes together in a pattern and, ta-da! You have a song.

Individual noises are called units.

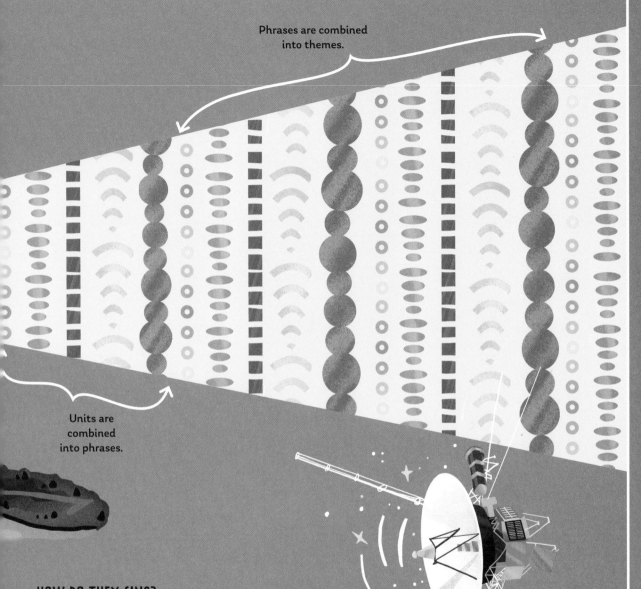

Phrases are combined into themes.

Units are combined into phrases.

HOW DO THEY SING?

To make noise, humpbacks first contract, or tighten, the muscles in their throat and chest. This squeezes air from their lungs across the vocal cords in their throat, which causes the vocal cords to vibrate, producing whale song!

WHALE SONG IN SPACE

In 1977 the Vogager spacecraft blasted off from Earth. On board were "Golden Records" containing sounds from our planet, including a humpback song from Bermuda. What piece of equipment do you think was used to record it?

MOTHERS AND CALVES

Baby whales, called calves, need their mothers to survive. Born on the breeding grounds, the calves are fed milk that is full of protein and fat by their moms, which makes them big and strong. During this period, which can last from six months to two years, the mothers teach their babies everything they need to know to survive in the ocean.

Female humpbacks only have one calf at a time.

HEADING DOWN

When calves are young, they hang out with their moms in shallow waters. As they grow and get older, their mothers take them to deeper waters.

TEACHING THE WAY

Once the calf is born, the mother whale pushes it gently up toward the surface so it can take its first breath. While mothers can come to the surface to breathe every 10 minutes, calves need to do so every 3–5 minutes.

STAYING CLOSE

Mothers and calves always stay within touching distance of each other. They even whisper to each other to make sure that predators like killer whales can't hear their conversations! When hungry, instead of calling out to its mom, the calf will simply rub against her to ask for milk.

Mother whales save energy by resting at the surface and breathing slowly.

21

BUBBLE NET FEEDING

Teamwork makes the dream work. Humpback whales have a clever trick they use when they want to catch fish: They work together to make a net!

CREATING THE NET

One whale swims in circles, releasing air from its blowholes to create a net of bubbles. Meanwhile the other whales swim around the net, trapping fish inside it!

OPEN WIDE!

The whale at the bottom waits for the right moment and then gives the command— time to eat! All the whales lunge upward at the same time with their mouths open. Only the lucky fish escape.

INSPIRED BY HUMPBACKS

EFFICIENT FLIPPERS

Look closely at a humpback whale's pectoral flippers and you'll notice that the front edges are very bumpy. These bumps are not just for decoration—they allow water to flow over the flippers more smoothly. This allows the whale to swim through the ocean more efficiently.

The bumps are called tubercles. Each whale has about 30–60 tubercles.

If we pay close attention to our surroundings, there is a lot we can learn. Inventors use the natural world—from animals to plants—to inspire them to solve problems and challenges. This is called biomimicry.

THAT GIVES ME AN IDEA...

Wind turbines use wind to make electricity. They are an important source of renewable energy. By adding bumps to the edges of the blades, scientists discovered that the blades could spin more easily and generate more electricity. It's all thanks to humpbacks!

The blades on a wind turbine look like humpback flippers.

Dr. Frank Fish invented this wind turbine.

WHALES IN DANGER

1 **NATURAL PREDATORS**

Orcas (killer whales) lurk around breeding grounds in the hope of finding a meal. They work together in a group to attack young and weak humpback calves, while the mothers try to protect them.

2 **ENTANGLEMENT**

Whales also often get entangled in fishing gear or nets that have been lost at sea. Many will drown, starve, or get infections from cuts caused by the nets. Entanglement is one of the biggest killers of whales.

3 **NOISE**

Whales use sound to find their way around the ocean. As ship traffic increases and the ocean gets noisier, humpback whales find it harder to speak to and hear one another. It's also hard to hear nearby predators or find their partners.

For whales, the ocean is one big obstacle course. They spend time avoiding both natural threats, like predators, and human-made threats, such as nets and ships. Let's learn more about the dangers humpbacks face on their journeys.

5

A polluted planet is bad news for humpbacks.

If you go whale watching, always respect the whales. They are wild creatures, not just objects for entertainment.

6

4

Whalers used harpoons to catch whales.

4 HUNTING

Many years ago, people used to hunt humpback whales for oil to light their lamps and to make butter. They used the baleen to make fishing rods. Luckily, humpback whales are no longer hunted on a large scale—although other whale species are.

5 CLIMATE CHANGE

As the ocean gets warmer due to climate change, the little creatures that humpbacks like to eat will move to different parts of the ocean. This means that the whales will be forced to follow their food to areas they're not familiar with.

6 SHIPS

Whales often travel through areas with a lot of ships. If boats get too close, they can hit and severely hurt whales. In the worst instances these collisions can kill humpbacks.

ECOSYSTEM ENGINEERS

Whales like humpbacks play an important role in maintaining the health of the oceans. In fact, whales are so important they're called "ecosystem engineers." This means whales have the power to create, change, and maintain the habitat (or ecosystem) in which they live.

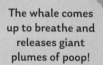

The whale comes up to breathe and releases giant plumes of poop!

THE WHALE PUMP

Whales helpfully transport useful nutrients, such as iron and nitrogen, from the deep ocean to the surface. These nutrients are released when the whale poops! Then they're used by phytoplankton (see right). This process is called the whale pump.

Whales dive deep to feed in places full of their favorite food and important nutrients.

Photosynthesis is the process in which plants convert sunshine into food for themselves (and oxygen for us).

WHALE CARCASSES

Dead whales are important food for many hungry species at the surface of our oceans. As they sink they also provide great feasts in the deepest, darkest parts where there is not as much food.

Sharks will happily munch on a whale's blubber.

PHYTOPLANKTON

Phytoplankton are tiny microscopic plants that live on the ocean's surface. They get energy from sunshine, as well as from ingredients like iron and nitrogen that are in whale poop. Then they release huge quantities of oxygen into the atmosphere. Did you know that every second breath of air you take is produced in the ocean?

Eel-shaped, slime-producing hagfish are big fans of dead whale!

GLOSSARY

Baleen
A comblike structure in the mouths of some whales, which they use to trap food.

Biomimicry
When people are inspired by nature to solve human problems.

Blowholes
Whale nostrils located at the top of the head and used for breathing.

Breaching
When a whale leaps out of the water.

Calf
Baby whale.

Dorsal fin
The fin on the back of a whale.

Ecosystem
All the living and nonliving things in an area. This includes animals and plants as well as rocks and soil.

Entanglement
To get caught up in fishing gear.

Hydrophone
An underwater microphone.

Krill
A small, shrimplike crustacean that floats freely with ocean currents.

Mammal
Warm-blooded animals with backbones (vertebrates) who have hair or fur and give milk to their young. Whales are mammals, and so are humans!

Marine biologist
A scientist who studies life in the ocean.

Migration
When an animal moves from one place to another at a certain time of year.

Nutrients
Substances in food that our bodies need to enable them to function properly.

Renewable energy
Energy that is made from resources that do not get used up, such as wind or sunshine.

Tail flukes
The boneless parts at the end of a whale's tail.

Tubercle
A fist-sized bump on a whale's head or flipper that is actually a hair follicle connected to a set of sensitive nerves.

Whale song
Melodic sounds made by male humpback whales.

INDEX

This has been a

NEON  SQUID

production

For Niam—thank you for giving me another reason to care for our oceans and their inhabitants. The ocean is vast and filled with magic—I cannot wait to explore it with you someday!

For Ammi and Thaththi—for always saying, "do what you love and you will do it well"—it worked!

Author: Dr. Asha de Vos
Illustrator: Jialei Sun
US Editor: Allison Singer

Neon Squid would like to thank:

Jane Simmonds for proofreading the book.

Copyright © 2022
St. Martin's Press
120 Broadway, New York,
NY 10271

Created for St. Martin's Press
by Neon Squid
The Stables, 4 Crinan Street,
London, N1 9XW

EU representative: Macmillan
Publishers Ireland Ltd,
1st Floor, The Liffey Trust Centre,
117–126 Sheriff Street Upper,
Dublin 1, D01 YC43

10 9 8 7 6 5 4 3 2 1

Library of Congress Cataloging-in-
Publication Data is available.

Printed and bound by Vivar
Printing in Malaysia.

ISBN: 978-1-684-49220-6

Published in June 2022.

www.neonsquidbooks.com